IF THE SKY IS AWAKE

KELVIN C. BIAS

ARCHIVE ZERO | NEW YORK | 2020
www.archivezero.com

Published by Archive Zero, LLC

Hardback ISBN: 978-1-7346603-0-2
Paperback ISBN: 978-1-7346603-1-9
E-book ISBN: 978-1-7346603-2-6

© 2020 by Kelvin C. Bias

Cover design by Robson Garcia Jr.
Cover photo: Kelvin C. Bias (Manhattan from the New Jersey side of the Hudson River, Jan. 11, 2011)
Formatting by Polgarus Studio

Names, characters, places, businesses and incidences either are the product of the author's imagination or used fictitiously, and any resemblance to actual persons, living or dead, businesses, companies, events, or locales is entirely coincidental.

No part of this book may be used or reproduced in any manner without written permission from the author, except in the case of brief quotations embodied in an article or a review.

'Ol' Rusty' first appeared in *Dime Show Review*, Volume 3, Issue 2 (2019)

PUBLISHER'S NOTE

What is Archive Zero?

The name is a combination of archive: a repository or collection, especially of information, and zero: (3rd definition) the point of departure in reckoning; more pointedly, the point from which the graduation of a scale (like a thermometer) begins.

When I created my own publishing company, I did so with the intent of trying to create a compendium of innovative content for the philosophers of the future. We are the architects.

According to Albert Einstein, any distinction between the past, present, and future is "a stubbornly persistent illusion." So perhaps if what's past is prologue, and the future is now, the present is both past and future, and a zero-point phenomenon occurs eternally. Envision all the words for human conditions that would look much better with the word "zero" in front of them.

War.

Famine.

Poverty.

Homelessness.

Prejudice.

The list could go on, but maybe one day, there will be no need for a list. In another way, my name could be read to mean: Absolute Zero (the Kelvin scale) Prejudice (Bias). Let's approach zero together.

Welcome to Archive Zero. Welcome to *If The Sky Is Awake*.

Kelvin C. Bias, Publisher, Poet, Philosopher

for the seekers

"We must learn to reawaken and keep ourselves awake, not by mechanical aids, but by an infinite expectation of the dawn."—**Henry David Thoreau**

Contents

BROKEN HUMAN 1
THE APRICOT TREE 3
THE LONG NIGHT 4
LET'S MAKE LOVE IN THE RIVER (OF LIFE) 5
THREE ITERATIONS OF I 6
ADVICE FROM A DEAD MAN 8
STANDING STILL ON ESCALATORS 10
IOWA 11
THE EXPLOSION 12
I WANT YOU 14
HARDWOOD 2000 16
DOMESTICITY 18
5:55 20
TO THE LADY AT THE APPLE STORE
    WTC 10:22 A.M. OCT. 1, 2019 21
WHY DID I SAY WHAT I SAID? 23
SOMEWHERE IN BROOKLYN 24
MONGOLIA 25
I AM 26
BROTHER CURTIS 29
IF THE SKY IS AWAKE 30
JUST DO AS I SAY 31
PROSTITUTED 32
SEXUAL PANACEA 34

SOCIAL MEDIARRHEA	36
MAN IN THE DUNES	38
IN THE AFTERMATH OF TOTAL DARKNESS	40
MONOTONY	41
GET PAID TO DAYDREAM	42
HEART-SHAPED PANCAKES ON NEW YEAR'S DAY	44
PURE BLUE	45
LETTERS AT 3 A.M.	47
BEING	48
PUMPKIN PIE	49
THE TOMB	50
PORN ON MARS	52
LEAVE SOMETHING BEAUTIFUL	54
IN THE ORBIT OF BEAUTY	55
WHEN I CAN'T REMEMBER A THING	57
BLUE-TIPPED MATCHES	59
TERRESTRIAL MAGNETISM	61
THE SOUND OF FALLING SNOW	63
DARK SPECK	64
FECHA	65
CINEMA	67
THE BLIZZARD	68
GHOST DESK	69
THE HAPPINESS OF EXPLICIT MEMORIES	71
FEEDING DUCKS IN ANTARCTICA	72
SAVING INK	74
LOVE AT 333 M.P.H.	76
BLACK SAND, BROWN FEET	77

THE TEST	78
ROTORUA	80
A CONVERSATION WITH AN ALMOST-THREE-YEAR-OLD LITTLE GIRL	82
YOU DON'T HAVE TO TELL ME "I LOVE YOU" AGAIN	84
SAILING TO ETERNITY	86
I DON'T EXIST IN THIS REALITY	90
NO ONE CARES IF YOU'RE SHAPELESS	93
TOO MANY PEOPLE	95
SUMMER OF '77	96
IMPUNITY	100
THE FAR SIDE OF TIME	101
WHERE DO LETTERS GO AFTER THEY'RE READ?	102
BLUE TEARDROPS	104
I FUCKING LOVE IT	106
THE COSMOS IS IN LINE AT IN-N-OUT	108
WET PAINT	110
THE FREEDOM OF A DARK BEDROOM	111
THE MUD PUDDLE	112
THE CONSTITUTION WILL NOT ENFORCE ITSELF	114
CITY OF CLONES	115
OL' RUSTY	116
LITTLE ETERNITIES	118
THE FIRST DEAD AMERICAN	120
RED LAMPSHADE AGAINST A DARK SKY	122
TWO HUMAN SOULS	125

FOREIGN-BODY SENSATION 127
THE LAST OPPONENT 129
ACKNOWLEDGMENTS 131
OTHER WORK BY KELVIN C. BIAS 133
ABOUT THE AUTHOR 137

IF THE SKY IS AWAKE

BROKEN HUMAN

I am a broken human.
I don't play well with others.
Narcissus is black like me.
People assume the worst,
Hope for the best,
Or crueler, the next collapse.
The next passed over.
The next shot 41 times.
The next "I can't breathe."
I am a man, flaws and all.
Unearthed on a blue world.
Dreams crushed.
Dreams rearranged.
Dreams trying to rise again.
Tests. Failure. Solitude.
The world has no pity.
The world is its own problem.
We litter. We burn. We chop down.
I cannot survey what I can't see.
I cannot see because my eyes are
Red with rage, brimmed with tears.
I'm choking on the detritus
Of perseverance. Yet still I mend.
Yet still I bend the ear.

Yet still I beat my heart.
Yet still I try.
Like a volcano, I bulge.
Hatred nullified by love.
I am a broken human.
Fusion in the confusion, constantly
Putting myself together again.

THE APRICOT TREE

Remember the voices,
The orange delectations
Hanging high, out of reach
From tiny brown hands.
But not out of the
Imagination.
They call to me.
Juicy, ripe, free.
Will they still be there
When I'm an old man?
A four-year old's fuzzy
Memory. Eating fallen
Fruit, not forbidden.
Minions and seeds.
The desert soil below.
Blue California sky,
Perched in the bounteous
Backyard of dreams.
Above, beyond, loved.
It hasn't rained in weeks.

THE LONG NIGHT

This is the gateway.
The words: a cipher.
An unlocked door appears.
Step through, naked in body
And strong will.
Enter the murky mind
Of the dreaming king,
The dreaming queen.
The dreaming dreamers.
You are in command.
Your head is resting on
A velvet pillow while
Your imagination swirls.
This is your new reality.
Last chance.
You enter. You're still here.
Minutes are hours.
Hours, eons.
Forever in a blink.
No spatial relations.
You are the God.
Illicit lovers, illicit sins.
Absolved. Fear, a
Distant master.
I'll join you.
There's a long night ahead.

LET'S MAKE LOVE IN THE RIVER (OF LIFE)

You, born a world away.
We, born of glacial decay.
Rivers formed, gliding
Toward the open sea.
Of lovers, of time, of possibility.
Destined to join.
Destined to be dammed.
Destined to overflow.
And longer still,
Destined for different deltas.
Until then, let's make love.
Let's dream. Let's hold dear.
A bigger river has us.
It has us all. Ingrained.
Look skyward.
And behold the rain.

THREE ITERATIONS OF I

I wish, I dream, I remember.
I am in awe of your eye.
I wish we had the time back,
The soft whisper of tingling skin,
Draped against one another
With nothing in between.
We dangle off the edge of the bed,
Rapturous, out of breath,
Are we dreaming?
Are we sleeping?
Are we on our last night on Earth?
Answers to unasked questions.
I do not wallow in the future.
I forever imagine the present,
Your gift, I appreciate your body.
And hope you appreciate mine.

I wish, I dream, I remember.
I am resplendent in our fantasy.
I dream about positions, potions,
Withholding nothing, coital,
In the throes of telepathic motion.
There is no bed. Only passion.
Our breaths breathe in unison,

Blowing rapidly in our furious wind.
Are we remembering?
Are we awake?
Are we ensconced in eternity?
We don't care about questions.
I do not bother with the past.
Your visions compliment mine.
Your body covers all my flaws.
Tomorrow is here, now, evermore.

I wish, I dream, I remember.
I am radioactive dust without you.
I remember only the bad,
Because it stings, bites, kills.
In the aftermath, there is no us,
Waiting to rejoin the fray.
The bed is plywood,
Rotting like an underwater pier.
Are we a mirage?
Are we sands in the desert?
Are we expectant dust?
I do not dwell in the present.
Your presence haunts me.
Your smell, perfume glistening,
Distraction: I hope we never forget.

ADVICE FROM A DEAD MAN

I am inside a black hole.
No light. No debate.
My body long since crushed.
At least I have my thoughts.
What shall I do with them?
Disseminate, divulge, dissuade
A protégé from passivity.
You'll be dead one day.
That pretty girl you want to kiss,
That distant land waiting to explore,
That signpost up ahead: the future?
There is none. There is only the
Infinite now. And on to the next.
Waiting is a form of fear.
I didn't follow my own advice.
I am in darkness. Wishing.
Each moment of my life
A pressure point on a timeline,
Scrubbed in an editing bay.
I am a man with no name,
Only a mane of longing regret.
Shed the crown, outward bound,
Before it's attained in Room X.
The whip and the rope,

And the chains we make for
Ourselves. Phantoms without
Power. All it takes is one.
Use your freedom and come undone.

STANDING STILL ON ESCALATORS

Stand to the right.
Right of the right
To ameliorate my progress.
Fill my mind with shocks,
Dodging the heels and
Power suits, and the man
Bellowing into a cell phone
While the world collapses.
Up, up and away.
Down, down, regulate.
Claustrophobic riffs,
Swept under the metallic maw.
I just want some exercise.
To fantasize as I pass the
Passersby. My morning
Process blinks in the eye.
I don't want the world
To remain still, to spend
Eternity on a loop.
Counteract the inertia.
Pass, run free. Escape
The movable beast.

IOWA

Alone with my thoughts.
Alone with others in the room.
Alone when surrounded by flowers.
Together when alone.
Together when unborn.
Together when minds cloned.
Answers elude me.
Beautiful smiles taunt me.
I stand at the edge of the firmament.
A figment of my own imagination.
Narcissism killed me dead.
Left me with nothing.
Save a pellet and some bread.
Selfish, gone, sad.
I must learn. To return
To the fulgent side of life,
To destroy my own strife.
Divined, divided, unseen.
Winter nights. Everclear.
If only a girl from Iowa.

THE EXPLOSION

The Big Bang.
The first of many.
A bridge to conflict.
A bridge to eternal
Ecstasy in an endless room.

A bridge collapsed,
Fallen into itself,
Reverberating.
Women, men.
Human beings.

Animals of life.
Organisms.
Engorged.
Blood pumped.
Volcanic sediment,

Resting in the corner.
On Earth's mantle.
Waiting to be opened.
Waiting to explode
Once more. Evermore.

Love is the universal
Origin. Loneliness.
Quenched.
Goodbye to the end.
It's just the beginning.

I WANT YOU

4:09 a.m. We are solitary.
The black rain pings the pane.
Creeping fluid separated by inches.
Glass dreams forged by desire.
I am your bidding man,
Your effervescent lover,
Perched at your command.
Tongues untied yet perfect
In rapturous grandeur.
We are a dream. I aim
For your thighs, divine Earth's
Gravity in your hips.
Two beasts hitched.
Pause. Slow. Temporal.
The night is ancient.
The night rules our connection,
Fuels delirious joy.
Your smile is the engine.
Our pleasure, raw,
Cooked how you please.
My digits entangled,
Exploring your dark beauty.
The rhythm, a syncopated beat
I want you to sing.

This *is* the next gig.
I want you. I want you. I want you.
Ask me something delicious.
I am happy to explain.
But first, this pace.
I continue to grow.
I am the book you
Don't want to put down.
The manual written for you.
The motions you prescribe.
I, the playful author,
Trying to maintain,
To hold back the flood.
The rain, the rain,
Soon, the deluge.
Soon, the exquisite gasps.
You *know* my weakness.
You know my strength.
You prop me up,
Pull my hands down.
You provoke insanity.
I dream of wild roots
Reaching toward Patagonia,
Horses galloping through
The halls of an institution.
We round up and around.
The cocked clock never stops.
I want you, I want you, I want you.
Infinity lopped.

HARDWOOD 2000

108th and Central Park West.
We know who we were.

A beautiful girl, a beautiful sight.
A beautiful man, a beautiful night.

Clothes strewn like rag dolls.
Us. Entangled. Enthusiastic lovers.

Kowtowing to passion on
An empty hardwood floor:

Our luscious playground,
A love paean. Naked poetry.

Standing, sitting, laying.
Words serve a lonely reminder.

I rely on memory, carrying
You from room to room.

We glide in and over one another.
In the dark shadows.

In the long night.
In the packed ambiance

Of welcome thrills.
No one before. No one since.

Rare, the telekinesis we share.
I hold your body tight.

I'm forever there,
Moaning for you in this utopia.

Upside down, sideways.
Steel, tall and proud.

You carve an indelible smile
On my face, in my soul.

I leak for days.
Panting, crying, shining,

Death-defying unwinding.
Secretions wiped and removed.

We stave the morning light,
Forgetting is harder still.

DOMESTICITY

I am a filthy dog.
A conduit of rage on
A rain-slicked Manhattan
Street. A firebrand
With no fire. Only an
Unlit fuse. I wish.
I hope. I confess.
I am a wandering blight,
A camouflage building
Oozing sadness,
Hemorrhaging desire.
Dishes unwashed,
Untouched by the rain
Like week-old trash.
Trying to become
Beautiful snow.
Blackness in the heart.
A small hole, metastasizing,
Atrophying hope.
I listen for a symphony,
A distant beacon in the
Night. A forgotten lover.
Someone else's memory.
Complaints piled high,

Rising glass and steel,
Forever on the move.
The City: The bane of
Domestic tranquility.
One foot in front
Of the other. I shuffle
Into my waking life
While a waft of steam
Drifts toward heaven.

5:55

Three numbers aligned,
Masters of my brain.
Alert. The guardian angel.
One more story, just one more.
The angel sleeps briefly,
Dreaming forever in an instant.
Mommy, the next...
"Daddy. Open the door please!"
Sadness unleashed into pitch black.
A light on. A light off.
A limbo of yells and half-awake
Decisions. All in the name of love.
All adored. All-knowing adulting.
The cries linger on a fleeting stage.
I hope they never subside.

TO THE LADY AT THE APPLE STORE WTC 10:22 A.M. OCT. 1, 2019

Your thin face bordered by
Luminous colors, dust whirled into
A frenzy and squeezed into a
White chenille top and a
Purple pencil skirt. You
Remind me of a distant friend.
A lover lost long ago on
Another continent, another mound
Of composite dust. What
Technological problem brought
You here? Someone didn't call you
Back and you realized your phone,
The tool of the ages, the extension
Cord of your life, operated on a
Different plane of non-operation?
Surrounded by other colors,
Other people, other clay
Configurations. Where crushed bones
Still lie. On the third day
We bow to the Apple god,
The magistrate of what we

Allegedly need. We are of the same
Ilk. Laptop and language out of sync,
Devices replacing physical
Connection, a finger touch:
Tantalum, lithium, screen
Protection. Projection of desire.
Let's throw stones at the glass.
You make the wait endurable.
Black hair, black bracelet dangling,
Within earshot of the woman
In the black Metallica T-shirt,
Black fishnets and black tattoos,
Beautiful too. She's gone now,
But we are all here, alone, together,
Buying, fixing, consuming.
Let's forget the backup.
The glitches and curses.
Your legs are exclamation points,
Your black heels, periods.
The white infinity is our friend.
10:59 a.m. She's gone too.
Despite this: new phone!

WHY DID I SAY WHAT I SAID?

The last words: the last supper,
Circulating in the methane-infused air.
Entrails of expletives mean little in
The space of sorrow, the anger
Of the quiet room as mosquitos hover.
Delete this hurtful pain unleashed.
Replace the void of silence; protect
Unperturbed angels in the other room.
Each night sound echoes in places
You dare not ask, feeding rumors,
Innuendos, somersaults fraught
With dog-eared contrivance.
The neighborhood listens.
Context: fleeting. Don't go to
Bed. Irresponsible cohorts,
Last-minute phone calls.
Why can't I retract action verbs?
The syllables, a dagger,
Engendering harm. In the end,
I am the one bleeding.

SOMEWHERE IN BROOKLYN

Somewhere in Brooklyn
Two lovers bicker.
Two planes subvert
The dark skies.
Lights fleeting into
Nothingness
As their passengers
Drift into dreams.
The playground is
Dormant. Cold wind
Replaces the laughter
Of children, stalking
The hardened streets.
There is no new year,
No vaunted answers
To life's mysteries.
Just a junked sofa and the
Ambient sounds of
Tomorrow.

MONGOLIA

The desert better-lived calls.
The Gobi. A ghost in my waking
Daydreams. The singing dunes,
The patient sky, its presence
More than enough.
A herd of yaks and sacred lakes.
Thoughts are all I have:
Inescapable truths.
Failure to resuscitate.
Failure to rebound.
Failure to revitalize.
Billowing cotton joins
The celestial parade.
A mirror to the snow-tipped
Peaks above the valley.
The smog of Ulaanbaatar
Vanquished in the wilderness.
I, the quarrelsome man, spurred
By 1,000 cuts. Small indignities
In the grand scheme
On the horizon. Blue,
My friend, stay with me.
Be my proverb.
Ground my existence
Before I rise.

I AM

I am pungent dust.
I am a force of will.
I am desperate thoughts.
I am myriad skill.
I am a word contortionist.
I am a walking contradiction.
I am nothing and everything.
I am an easy reader.
I am a difficult lover.
I am a great father.
I am a terrible husband.
I am an amazing husband.
I am a bad dad.
I am a fervent sinner.
I am cold as ice.
I am in a place in time.
I am time in another place.
I am a figment of my imagination.
I am a fragment of a soul.
I am the embodiment of it all.
I am a religion.
I am a curdled cult.
I am wallowing on the floor.

I am not an idol.
I am not a tall tree.
I am not a brown cow.
I am not the fusion of atomic destruction.
I am not proud of myself.
I am not the President.
I am not speaking in tongues.
I am not the master of my domain.
I am not captain of the high seas.
I am not who you think I am.
I am not a poet.
I am not a teacher.
I am not a gun owner.
I am not a disciple.
I am not a distant relative.
I am not the fallen sky.
I am not a shining star.
I am not seeking buried treasure.
I am not patient.
I am not a good listener.
I am not the father.
I am not the son.
I am not a ghost.

I am full of joy.
I am angry.
I am ready to listen.
I am experiencing growing pains.

I am pained to say I know little.
I am in awe of the oceans.
I am in sprawl to it all.
I am an alien on a foreign world.
I am in need of shelter.
I am lowly beneath the tides.
I am an undertaker of sadness.
I am madness in a maelstrom.
I am a deacon consecrating birth.
I am basking in the shadows.
I am weather under the sun.
I am seeking pleasure.
I am hopeful in the face of darkness.
I am blessed by three angels.
I am battling hate.
I am overflowing with love.
I am neither here nor there.
I am kissing the future.
I am what I am.

BROTHER CURTIS

Flow, flow, flow.
The river of rhythm,
The soul of soul.
Reach the sky.
Preach. Teach. Learn.
Up, up, up.
Syncopation never dies.
We move to your beat.
We move in your heat.
Scars, tears, wiped clean.
Paradise is in your voice.
In our ears, in our
Collective experience,
Infinite drums, no B side.
Forever and a way,
We smile, smile, smile.
Across Brooklyn and beyond.
You will never fade.

IF THE SKY IS AWAKE

Logic from the connoisseur of dawn.
Beautiful curls frame her eyes,
The knowing intent.
Wisdom flows.
Five years. Five lifetimes
In a sentence. Her declaration:
You cannot sleep when the sky is awake.
It shrieks across the room like a flame.
Philosophy and air.
Morning born. The gray
Between dark and light.
How will you guide the sun?
Memories will always be there.
The Elemental Four Tops:
Earth, Air, Fire, Water.
Remember childhood.
Stand prepared,
Marinating in possibility.
If the sky is awake,
We are too.

JUST DO AS I SAY

Nobody listens to me.
Just do as I say and
There will be no problems.
So you want a robot?
Don't talk to me.
That's a good idea.
Just do what I ask
When I ask it. Right away.
Now? What did you say?
Don't be a smart ass.
You can dish it out but
You can't take it.
You have no right to complain.
Stating a fact is not complaining.
You're such a hypocrite.
I can't express my thoughts?
I do everything around here.
And of course I do 100% nothing.
I don't want to talk to you anymore.
It's pointless. You better learn.
Can we end this ongoing conversation?
Stave magistrates and condemnation?
Just do as I say.

PROSTITUTED

I have too much ego
And not enough spice.

I have too much morality
And not enough vice.

Quick satiation
Bleed, bleed, bleed.

Those tears won't do
Anyone any good.

The oldest profession:
Some say it's a sin.

Cocks up, lips splurged.
Decisions splayed in agony.

Of deviant curves.
The notion is against

My fragile constitution
Yet I cannot convict

The temptation.
Sometimes we need a

Sensation. A prick.
A time, a place.

A season, if you wish,
A nudge in the wrong

Direction to set us on
A glorious path.

To keep fires lit.
All done in the proper light.

In the open. In the mind.
Without blinding your wit.

SEXUAL PANACEA

Throbbing, longing
Throbbing pain.
The cure is sex.
The ease to all ills.
Stress free, sheets' glee.
The couple on the platform,
Arguing about family
During the holiday.
When did they last hold hands?
When did they last lock lips?
When did eyes roll back?
Hips swayed in every direction.
Mind relaxed. Numb to the shame.
Let's examine the delicacies:
Anxiety, memory fades,
Immunity implodes, resentment
Rises, cancer creeps inside.
The longer it goes,
The longer the woes.
Make love for God's sake!
Make meaningful moans
And leave all residue
At the graveyard of unhappiness.
Safely. Slowly. Slippery.

This is it. This is you. This is me.
Time to fly, cry no more.
We will make you believe.
We will make you achieve.
A permanent smile desires
Eternity. Fuel engorged wishes.
Amen! Amen! Amen!

SOCIAL MEDIARRHEA

Like this. Post that.
Thumbs up. Thumbs down.
Everybody drown.
Nobody cares. Nobody shares.
The sickness that leaves
Us on the sidelines.
Losing water, losing weight.
A tool, it can be divine.
A way to connect,
A way to love, yet alone.
Mind the sleight of hand,
The glow of a smartphone
In a twisting void.
Trolls? They don't exist.
Someone you'll never meet,
A ghost in a world engine,
A typhoon striking nowhere
Except your own mind
Where the insidiousness spreads.
Drink lots of water:
Spend time with friends,
Milk cows in the dead of winter,
Let the sun shape your face,
Kiss your daughters,

Laugh as you ponder the redwoods
Without telling the world
The exact spot, the precise longitude,
Count with an abacus,
Share a bed with an accomplice,
See Corcovado, don't take a picture.
Forget the bucket list.
Feel. Touch. Breathe. Salivate.
It doesn't matter what you think.

MAN IN THE DUNES

I will not see the future
Until I climb the tallest dune.
To survey the Sea of Japan.
Its surface, glass,
A mirror reflecting
Earthly cinema.
The air is still, the sands
Absorbing the undisturbed tide.
The hidden sun belies the signs
Warning of its glory,
Its power to conquer.
It was a good day to come,
My wife says. A time for a
Dreamer latent in Teshigahara's
Playground. A black ant
In someone else's picture.
Summer gray created by
Tomorrow's clouds.
I am a foreign man,
But not in a foreign land.
Tottori waited for me.
Waited for my family.
Daughters' laughter
Welcoming the wind.

We too, pose, squeezed
Between the remains of
Crustaceans long past
And the radiant creatures
Poised to witness
A boundless sunrise.

IN THE AFTERMATH OF TOTAL DARKNESS

Quietus: The final frontage
Road? Or the destination?
I do not know the answer.
Many claim to know.

Others force others to know.
Billions place faith in no fear,
Knowing they will go elsewhere.
There are many ways to discover.

Is there only one finality?
We were born of darkness.
Will it not be the same
Upon our assured demise?

The scariest notion of them all:
Infinite nothingness.
In the aftermath, our bath,
Our glide into knowing unknowing.

MONOTONY

I'll stop bitching and moaning
If you stop bitching and moaning.
Words, like vomit, purged.
They needed to be said.
They needed to be heard.
They needed to be written.
The monotony of argumentation
Is not a celebration. An amalgam
Of repetitive motions does not
Stop the merry-go-round.
The chains we place muddy
The roiling waters. Shame:
To be the same, to appear lame,
To dance under a night, tame.
If we exist differently tomorrow,
Will it still end the same way?
Storms intercede, cloning closure,
Adding to the excitement,
Temporarily, then recede.
Vanquished to return again.

GET PAID TO DAYDREAM

Get paid to daydream.
I read it somewhere.
A banner on the subway
Methinks. A deposition.
They weren't upset
When they wrote it.
They, the ubiquitous they,
Dreaming once, beating
Heart riled in the city.
Today they are you and me.
Straphangers on the L train
On a rainy day, shy of a new year.
I notice each withered face.
Rush hour. Each plucked fantasy.
The woman carting her clear plastic
Bag brimmed full of more plastic,
Seltzer, Coca-Cola, Poland Spring.
Aluminum peppered inside.
Budweiser, Diet Coke.
Beads of liquid match those
On the black linoleum floor.
I exit somewhere in Williamsburg.
Utterly on the grid.
A red dot on a screen.

I course the slicked street.
Wondering what happened to
That girl in the fifth grade:
Denise Wong. Told me I looked
Like Jamaal Wilkes. Maybe
She's on a beach somewhere
In Thailand. Or sun-drenched sand
In Namibia. I wander still.
Now in line to pick up a pill.
Doctor make the pain go away.
Infections are infectious.
Chefchaouen, the Blue City,
Is only a flight away.
Places I conjure, hope to view.
Don't let the thoughts fade.
Write them down, draw them up.
Twenty paces, the drone is home.
I still haven't made a cent.

HEART-SHAPED PANCAKES ON NEW YEAR'S DAY

Washing dishes is inherently enraging.
New Year, new you.

The piled detritus in the sink remains.
I posit a solution, the remedy

Ripe like a Dr. Seuss concoction.
Make some heart-shaped pancakes.

Simple batter, a strawberry or two,
Lick your fingers and, whoosh,

The strain flies away.
The healing begins with

The mesmerizing mixture on the grill,
Spatula in hand the moment

Golden brown becomes perfection.
Flip. Repeat. Enjoy.

Make some heart-shaped pancakes.
The china will be sweet.

PURE BLUE

Fishing for blues
I open a book,
Or browse a page.
I dive into the deepest sea.
Seeking answers.
Seeking pleasure.
Seeking uncommon company.
An imaginary wordsmith,
Reading a letter in her dark boudoir.
Our blue moment-—nine definitions.
Her skin. Let me count the ways:
1. Of the color of the sky. We lay naked beneath Earth's shield.
2. Bluish: the color of a bruise. Gently attained in a clutch of passion. A sudden fall onto the carpeted floor. Vigorous action.
3. Our spirits are low. The lack of intimacy is depressing. Nothing more needs to be said.
4. Wearing the shade. A blue suit all week. What eyes will notice? Minds brimmed with fantasies of their own choosing.
5. A well-informed woman. Less fear, we are unrepentant lovers. She knows everything and what we both like. She possesses answers to all questions

      and asks none in return.
6. Puritanical laws on Sunday. We will not abide.
7. A profane hue. We wallow in our depravity, a seaman and a mermaid fully enthralled.
8. Singing the blues. My lady done up and left me.
9. Vote Blue. The donkey liberally pulls the levers.

These are the signs of archaic desire,
Reborn in the azure eyes of another.
Somebody is going to get a good blue streak.
The kind that lasts and leaves stains.
In its place, leavening for the thing we need.
I am on a quest to remain on this roiling ocean,
One big soup of wondrous aquatica,
Ballooning with the waste of heartbreak.
We crave a filter, a panoply of every meaning.
What life deals is pure.

LETTERS AT 3 A.M.

Words have an inclination.
A destination. Perceived
Without tribulation in the curves
Of your delicious mind.

The fog rolls in as I write.
Fantasies stenciled on *my* brain,
Rising to the level of concern.
Sinking to the depths of forgetting.

I imagine your kaleidoscopic room,
Who was last there?
Dream together, separately.
We are the only ones who see.

Bound for the mailbox,
Bound for oblivion?
Silence. Where lovers reside
When answers come.

BEING

I haven't always been angry.
I've loved, laughed and looked
At lewd photos, smiled,
Then become sad.
I haven't always been melancholy.
I've burst into cheers. Mr. Glad.
I haven't always been happy.
I've shed copious tears.
It's no mystery: I am transforming.
From one second to the next.
One state of being to another.
Particles, malleable, like minds.
I haven't always been lonely.
I've been crushed by humanity.
I haven't always been a friend.
I've listened to an endless ring.
I haven't always been careful,
But I've always been.

PUMPKIN PIE

An orange mélange of sweetness,
Radiating from the pan of life.
Nothing wills more than the willing.
I don't want it to end.
Your skin reminds me of the taste.
The sheer happiness, unwise yet pure,
As if speeding on that Bolivian curve.
Methods of mitigation
Do not stand a chance.
I want to consume you like pumpkin pie.

THE TOMB

There is no messiah.
No rock covering the exit,
A long-ago entrance to prestige.
The forlorn workers,
Diligent at the height of their glory,
There is no one now.
Only the silent cubicles,
The rows of empty chairs,
Formerly filled with the laughter
Of clacking fingertips and
The freedom of the press.
They lie, unfettered, like
Headstones without inscriptions.
Lies rule, and rue, the day.
The shadowed carpets shrink
Into the cloying distance,
Dust their dance partner.
The swivel-back seats remain lucid,
Forming a darkened menagerie
Of mismanaged, downsized grief.
A light flickers as a winter sunset
Blinds the watcher, Lady Liberty,
Keeping vigilant witness
While streaks of orange

Try to save the day.
Once a media circus,
Today a mausoleum
For the Fourth Estate.
Buyouts and empty drawers,
Ghosts of timecards past.
The rays peek deeper,
Seeking a cohort of their own.
Alas, there is nobody here.
Nobody left to tell the tale.
Save for printing plates and
Elevator banks, bound for hell.

PORN ON MARS

How will the inaugural orgasm on Mars occur?
The first human explorer to act human,
To return to their base, engage in their
Base desires, splurge on a digital Goddess/God.
Perhaps alone at the same time.
Or in no time with the same unfulfilled dream.
An android lover programmed to oblige?
Semen on a New Tijuana bible,
Cleaned up by an Earth immigrant.
A job nobody wanted to do.
The human element, we must contend.
A flesh shell augmented by porn?
Robots, yourself and others.
They are the architects of pleasure.
Will the U.S. Space Force regulate love,
Shower the Red Planet in its rusty glory?
Delayed from Paris, New York, Tokyo.
Who will be the true star?
This beautiful figure used to keep the
Mission going, to breathe still.
Stand your lover up with one foot
On the floor and the other
Reflected in a virtual mirror.
Will it into existence.

Throw your lust into the mix.
Grin, twirl, the naked alliance.
Somebody has to do it.

LEAVE SOMETHING BEAUTIFUL

The hours pass unaffected.
Tomes gather dust on the shelf
While time passes into old age.
Solitaire is a nameless flame.
Its memory dictating action.
Clutch passion when it's in your grasp.
Hold tight, let fires burn.
Perfection lurks everywhere,
In the deeds of desire.
Create life forms before your form fades,
Before the amniotic chance breaks.
Upend the sun and rotate,
Muscles like horses
In a contortionist's court.
Grab one, grab all.
Bosoms and voices.
Bodice on ice, your body lean,
Peering into the frosty distance.
Condensation, a witness.
Our magnificent birthday suits.
We are the legion of love,
A battalion of two,
Leaving something beautiful.

IN THE ORBIT OF BEAUTY

This fable needs a setting.
Yes, a mountain meadow,
Blossoms falling like embers
In the alpine air.
The sky opens and opines,
Where is the beauty?
The aspens bend toward the wind.
An answer swells in the crooked
Branches, pinnacles aimed for
Their inquisitive friend.
She has a name, the willows join in
Unison with the babbling streams,
Water destined for the sea.
Foam builds in the absence of snow.
Confined to the edges of rushing
Life. Salmon bow their heads.
They, too, repeat the mantra:
She has a name.
She has a nubile form,
A figure from a painting.
Mother Nature rises as if a dream.
Her fury, her gorgeous charm,
The stillness we never notice.
Listen to the narrator.

He will fail in his attempt.
Fail in his desire to capture
Her essence. Is it you?
The sky spins while the
Sounds of Earth
Circle the heavens.
She has a name.
She has a name.
She has a name.

WHEN I CAN'T REMEMBER A THING

You are a human being,
On a planet named Earth.
I don't know if you can see,
Hear, make love, start wars.
All of the above?
You are flesh and blood,
And crying isn't a thing.
The courage to try is everything.
Find some old videos, look at the smile,
Your daughters, plural,
Hypnotized by their gleaming eyes.
Recreate the Eiffel Tower.
Take off your clothes and shout
Naked at the top of your lungs
From the ledge of the building,
Scaring people. People without
The inner knowledge you possess.
They don't know your humorous bone.
They think you will jump.
Don't plummet, but feel the rushing air.
Then go back inside and wonder where
You are. You are somebody.

You have a name.
Ask to see your ID.
Then kick over a bucket,
Wink at the pretty nurses,
And drool over some pumpkin pie.
For this simple fact:
It won't be on your tombstone.

BLUE-TIPPED MATCHES

There, on the morning sidewalk
Astride a bold crack,
A peculiar device,
Dishing chemical advice,
Unleashed from the wrong
Hands. A band of blue
Atop a wooden bane,
An entryway, a gateway drug,
An inner voice barely audible.
Don't strike it. Come clean.
Somebody lost their will here
After a clean smoke,
Or a brazen night
Of ecstasy, during
Their walk of shame.
Curious objects bereft of breath.
Inanimate, but powerful.
Animate your world with
This power to burn it down.
A steppingstone to greater bombs.
Bigger devices. Bigger budgets:
The military industrial complex.
Left by and for cavemen,
Fight fire with fire. Kill. Inflame.

Or take another path.
Fulfill a liberal destiny.
Light the mind instead.
A gentle man of some age
Watches readily from the steps
Of the old folk's home.
Put it back, young man,
The sad-tipped matches
Are no match for you.
And then it starts to rain.

TERRESTRIAL MAGNETISM

Voiceless: 3:03 a.m. in New York City.
Palindrome on a dime.
Dignified, you've landed at Narita.
I alone in a different atmosphere,
Swirling within my own fantasy.
The winter air, cool, wafting in
From the open window, cloaks the
Heat you elicit. The ethereal
Connection, among two terrestrial
Brethren. Longing, desire, health,
I wish you all three.
I wish you my body.
You wish me yours.
We imagine in a different dimension.
Envision a friction without division.
Symbiotic visions rendered beneath
Earth's force field. Protection,
In your arms, your beautiful skin,
Your lips, my chest.
Your thighs, my unrest.
Beings on the same wavelength.
Manifesting unconquered hopes,
The wonders we've never experienced.
Warmth generating a fever sting,

A sweet torture I wish to quench,
To compulsively jettison.
So our world can keep on spinning.
I am naked, toes pointed to Tokyo,
Hands holding an imaginary armrest.
We take flight and forget our names.
Even though we haven't connected
In this plane, this outbound lifetime,
I harbor a dream in your eyes.
Up, up, up. Prone clouds moan.
All for the sake of perfection,
We must keep the globe grinning.
Our magnetism, our ecstatic prison.

THE SOUND OF FALLING SNOW

It used to be January around these parts,
The window sill a temple to a
Family of cardinals. Nested,
Until they vanished, aware of
The coming winter disappearance.

Their neon red feathers had no place
In the new status quo, no *raison d'etre*.
Stark blood against an undying field.
Cold heat in the midst of time.
We only see them in pixels now.

Digital images captured and fed
Into the master computer.
I remember the sound of falling snow.
Silence like no other. Save extinction.
Nowhere is safe. No map secure.

Blast your L-train headphones
Until you can't because
Earth's bathtub overflowed.
Next stop: Evaporation. Hark,
Welcome to Venus.

DARK SPECK

Are you a dark speck in
Somebody else's painting?
Or are you creating
Your own masterpiece?
Do colors drop from
The life you're curating?
Do rainbows fill your skies?
Is your horizon upside down?
Or are there other specks?
A tapestry filled with opportunity,
Things we all delight?
Is there a community of artists?
Of patrons? Of tomorrow's
Sunrises? Yes, I shout.
Yes, yes, yes!

FECHA

Hecho en Mexico.
Aztec Eagles
Soaring long ago.
Their contributions
In the second war
To end all wars,
Lost to history,
Like stale cheese.
Too bad: I like
Pottery and flan.
Cafe con leche.
Eggs and chorizo too.
When did *my*
Country's milk
Go bad? Look
At the date
For clues.
July 4, 1776? No.
Expired 11/8/16.
That explains a
Different birth.
It doesn't unravel
The children in cages,
The lack of humanity,

The vitriolic furor
Spawned and spewed
At "rallies".
The voter suppression,
The propaganda and lies.
Don't look at the
Numbers on a
Plastic jug,
The cruel cries of
"Mexico will pay."
Look at the calendar.
Election Day is
Everyone's date.

CINEMA

How many girls did I
Miss a kiss because
I actually cared about
The movie? *Le cinéma*.
Superseding all.
An exhibition of love,
An examination of life,
A never-ending party.
Your theater, my palace.
An indescribable feeling.
An unpacked Dream.
Joy in the dark.
Television is a box.
My dad said idiots
Live there. And we all
Know: You can't
Kiss a girl while
Sitting next to your
Parents on the sofa.

THE BLIZZARD

The sky, blue in the aftermath,
Clean from mankind's hand.
A plane of clouds in the distance
Shears the remains of humanity.
Nature's fury approaches.

I am a polar bear.
Wandering the streets of
An extinct city.
On a solemn journey
Through immortal winter.

The last of my species,
A green torch breaks the ice,
Fallen on its side. Gently.
We commune in the twilight
Before the blizzard cries.

GHOST DESK

Varnished wood,
A reddish hue shy of
2 a.m., beyond shuffling feet,
Vanished on a corner,
Disappearing into the dark.
A desk with no author.
She needs a shadowy
Figure to borrow her charms,
To scare a solitary passerby.
Undeterred, I stop and admire.
Streetlights reflected
On her smooth surface,
Where manuscripts
Once born, were then
Sent into the world
Of ideas and found glory.
Her former owner,
Vanquished. Tired
Of an oblong drawer
Two sizes too big.
Shreds of evidence
Are hard to procure
Under the cover of night.
As are reasons for

Her ghostly stare.
I hope she's there
Come morning.

THE HAPPINESS OF EXPLICIT MEMORIES

Tomorrow is tomorrow is tomorrow.
Memories are the future. Focus on today,
The dripping sweat from your lover's body.
Bend, circulate, ambulate, penetrate.
Words into action, nearing satisfaction.
The ogre of aggression flees in the throes,
Banished to a distant land: the past.
The immediacy of now is your ally.
Take a chance, ask for what you desire.
The happiness of knowing will ply you either way.
Take an expressive bath, a knowing voyage,
To places your lecherous soul imagines.
Create reveries of gliding birds,
Phantoms of pleasure higher than Cloud 9,
In the furthest reaches of this circulating globe,
Dune 7, McMurdo Station, Diego Garcia,
Carnal teachers in every corner.
All lie still in the aftermath of ecstasy.
Tomorrow is an explicit remembrance.
I'm happy for the sexual angels we share.
Here. Now. Today.

FEEDING DUCKS IN ANTARCTICA

When the calendar has no meaning,
There will be a final reckoning.

A drawing of lots to determine
Which radiation-ravaged land

Gets to relocate to Terra Incognito.
To take their chance among the

Evanesced icebergs, the flamingoes and
Other fowl making a new migration.

The last surveyors can't keep up,
Their maps obsolete by the hour.

When all compasses point South,
The bottom of the world will rule.

No need for fire. Erebus power.
Social Engineers attempt another dome,

A spaceport, a place to commune
Until they build a new mothership,

Assembled over generations.
A futile vessel to save them

While they ascribe, emaciated, to
New rules for a new country: U.S.A.

The United States of Antarctica.
Where citizens feed ducks while they die.

SAVING INK

Op-Ed. Drop dead.
Protests and Protestants.

Everyone has two cents.
Megaphones, Internet,

Twitter, Instagram.
Flip flop. It's all a sham,

A dredging of hate,
Of what we think we like.

Sure, social media
Saves ink, but what

Demons does it foment?
Quit searching for Wi-Fi.

Build the ever-present next
Wonder of the World.

Sign your name on
The dotted line?

No thank you.
My contract is in my mind.

It roils hearts and inspires.
Someday I'll write it down.

LOVE AT 333 M.P.H.

You are beyond my control.
In your alluring presence,
I become a drag racer,
Speeding toward oblivion
At 333 m.p.h. Naked,
Devious thoughts bared.
Stop lights and stop signs,
And other warning devices
Are of no avail. I am a
Heat-seeking missile,
Happily homed on your lips,
A driver without a seatbelt,
Helmet or morals.
Your hips, a fireball.
Then the slow burn.
Engine revved for
A concupiscent continuation.
I am overwhelmed.
Destined for a vanishing point.

BLACK SAND, BROWN FEET

Black sand, brown feet.
Black man, brown eyes.
I walk alone on a frosty
Icelandic morning.
Reynisdrangar, my guide.
Blonde hair a present memory.
Different lives on different paths.
If, at once, a fleeting ecstasy.
Lying nude, after making a wish,
In a roadside lodge somewhere
In the recesses of my imagination.
Was it a dream?
Sliding inside from behind,
Blind to the obvious obstacles.
A glimpse at other passions.
It could have been Vienna.
It could have been Barcelona.
It could have been,
Like footsteps on the beach.
Gone before I had a
Chance to walk away.

THE TEST

I failed your test.
I knew then. I know now.
I was raised to escort a woman
Home at the end of the night.
Same sweater, different guys.
Brunch? I was confused.
Was I supposed to mention
The indignity? I let it slide.
Another moment of clarity
Of which I was aware:
It was tests, plural.
Maybe I had a few more
Chances than most.
Or you were being kind.
I didn't want to be doing
Laundry on Sunday night either.
Tears alone at the airport Monday.
Four hours before my flight.
I wanted to pass an exam
On a Norwegian mountain in May.
Not running out of gas
On a Frankfurt hill.
Or maybe I should have
Purchased that Hugo Boss suit.

Wear it in a movie someday
Instead of carrying the ghosts
Of things I failed to do.

ROTORUA

The Waikato, beset
With verdancy
And azure skies,
Winds through
The creases hidden
Within my cranium,
Meeting other rivers,
Other remembrances of
Things past, past their
Target date, past their
Unachieved future,
Creating new tributaries
In other minds,
Leading to greater
Dreams and worlds,
Leading to other pastures,
Waters filled with life,
Washing the mud of
Rotorua into ancient artifacts.
New Zealand calls again,
A Māori greeting,
A cold Lion Red,
A different wife,
A river, gaining ground,

Pacific drainage,
I am newfound,
Like Captain Cook,
A figure of maritime history,
A man I can never meet,
Yet I broach new sails.
And as the salient grey mud
Remains, spewing air bubbles
To the surface,
I am an admiral,
Dredging my own sea clay.

A CONVERSATION WITH AN ALMOST-THREE-YEAR-OLD LITTLE GIRL

Do you want to go to the park?
I don't like going to the park.
(a split second later)
I want Cooper Park.
I don't like a different park.

Why don't you like a different park?
I want Cooper Park.

What's so special about Cooper Park?
No, I want Cooper Park,
I don't like different park.

Are different parks not as good as Cooper Park?
I want to be Cooper Park, okay?

What's the best thing about Cooper Park?
Um....um. *Frozen*.
I want *Frozen II*.
Where's Elsa?
Daddy, I want Elsa.

Let's go to Cooper Park.
No, I want Elsa.
I don't like Cooper Park.

You just like to say I don't like it.
(a sly little girl grin)
It's TV time.
(when the *Frozen* title credits roll)
Beautiful.

YOU DON'T HAVE TO TELL ME "I LOVE YOU" AGAIN

The morning din of backpacks,
Screeching chairs, knapsacks
Dropped on the floor.
Greetings and salutations.
Red table, blue table, green table.
In 50 years nobody will remember.
Some of the little hearts won't
Remain to share the memory.
Worry: the plinth of parenting.
Kissing your child goodbye,
Lingering in their joyous embrace.
Your angel's voice rises above the others.
Don't go. I want to stay with you.
Nevertheless, there are protocols.
You know you must leave.
You head for the open door.
You turn, seeking your tiny face,
Your blood, your DNA and love.
You blow a kiss and whisper:
I love you, one more time.
Certainly not the last?
Her eyes meet yours, Daddy's pride,

Burning to affirm the obvious.
You don't have to tell me
"I love you" again, she says.
The meaning is clear.
And you walk through that open door,
Eagerly awaiting tomorrow's encore.

SAILING TO ETERNITY

A single chord glides over a quiet sea,
Radiates without a compass
Into the perpetual unknown.

It is a drop in the universe,
Gone in a blink, but not without
Ripples, extending evermore.

Silence returns. Ready to abate.
A dark ship sails toward its cargo
Through sentient waters.

Colorful smoke springs
From her bellows, eclipses
The dissipating fog.

A leeward visitor veiled in white
Stands on the shore,
Raising a withered hand,

Without need of a coin,
Love, cloistered in her
Shrouded visage.

You emerge on the foredeck,
Ascend to the crow's nest, while
A louder chord strikes

From an unseen organ.
Is the sky the one playing?
There is no captain,

No guiding orders.
The wind of Elysium
Is in formal command.

You alone interpret the rhythms,
As longer chords join others,
Souls rapturous in their desire

To make themselves heard.
Your clipper, the Flying Cloud,
Pinpoints the black sand.

You drop anchor and
A rowboat, carry yourself
To the woman, drawn

By the symphony of solace.
The breaking waves quicken.
Unafraid, you step into the

Salty din, mesmerized by
The woman's song.
It was not the sky, or an organ.

It was her voice, disembodied.
Her bony hand emerges from
A white robe, takes yours.

You are coupled, known
To each other from a previous
Journey in another world,

Bound by an inexplicable bond.
You stand tall and finally see
A fleshless face, a knowing skull.

You kiss. A distant lighthouse
Blows a horn. Her hands
Cradle your naked body, reborn.

Your flesh becomes hers.
As your bones dry,
Turn to dust, white residue perches

On grains blacker than Night.
The new woman kneels before
Your remains, then traces

The whispers of your aura
Into your image, into your carnage.
New flesh coagulates,

Oozing upward into your new body.
A beautiful blue rises too.
Countless shades, the comrades

Of the ship's smoke,
Form a landscape of peace.
You hold the woman's hand.

Her name is Eternity,
Your lover, your guide
Into the next phase of exploration.

The Flying Cloud, moored on
The shoals of paradise, waits until
You need her again.

I DON'T EXIST IN THIS REALITY

I don't exist in this reality.
My mind doesn't wrap itself around this world:
The world where brown countries are bombed,

The world where my vote doesn't matter
Because of a slave owner's Electoral College,
The world where my name is purged

From the voter roll, the world that commits
Sins in the name of guns and religion,
The world that keeps children in cages,

The world that heats up to kill the
Virus that infects it, the world where
Two lovers of a different stripe get

Stopped and stared, frisked and searched,
A world where propaganda is beloved,
Believed and hailed by the chief, a world

Where mine eyes have seen the glory
Of the coming of the slum lords,
A world where the first shall be first and

The last shall remain last, a world where
Black men are wrongly convicted, while
The other man stands his ground, a world

That will only pass gun control when
There is no one left to shoot, a world
We are told is fair. I am not of this reality.

I plan another world: The world where
The person with the most votes wins,
A world where more trees are planted

Than video game schematics, a world where
People are only allowed to hunt
On an empty stomach, unless they want

To have their big-game belly mounted on the wall
In the lion exhibition at the zoo, a world
Where synagogues, churches and mosques

Are not targets, a world filled with lush
Forests in the Amazon, not nuclear bombs,
A world with arguments and called witnesses,

A world where everyone's vote matters, a
World with no military industrial complex,
Only complex thinking to solve complex

Problems, provide sustainable life, a world
Where someone can love as they choose
Without being banished from the home, a

World with a clock nowhere near midnight,
A world where fossil fuels fuel nothing
But a paleontologist's chisel, a world

With zero war, poverty, famine, hate,
Zero concerns, a world we won't have
To leave for another one, a world filled

With love, healthy laughter and thought,
A world, in short, that doesn't lie or die
And we can all exist there: in reality.

NO ONE CARES IF YOU'RE SHAPELESS

Faceless, nameless, shameless,
Wandering the streets aimless.
A chameleon changing pages.
Sidewalks and sewers, able rages.
No one cares if you're shapeless.

Faceless, nameless, shameless
Discarded food ain't contagious.
The night warrior seeking retribution.
Your spirits, your constitution.
No one cares if you're shapeless.

Faceless, nameless, shameless.
Watch where you're going Mr. Anxious.
The graffiti guides your soleless shoes.
The moon, the girls, the milieu,
No one cares if you're shapeless.

Faceless, nameless, shameless.
Maybe a vagabond can fix this mess.
Heat shafts and rafters, pills,
Dodging the hustlers, the conscious shrills.
No one cares if you're shapeless.

Faceless, nameless, shameless.
Sneeze into your sleeve, God bless.
All it takes is one to take note.
The denizens of Manhattan passing, rote.
No one cares if you're shapeless.

TOO MANY PEOPLE

The Dutchman?
Eternity has nothing on the L.
Like Tokyo and the running
Of the bulls. A girl gored me
With her breakup tears.

Morning inglorious.
Everyone was on the same train,
Listening to something other
Than the mumbled jumble of
The motorman's instructions.

Next stop Union Square.
Everyone got off and left
Peace in the air. A Post-It
Note monument, the only witness.
Too many people. Handle with care.

SUMMER OF '77

Dodge Aspen, silver and blue.
The Ship of Dreams on an enchanted
Voyage across a continent:

United States of America.
L.A. to Niagara.
Mom and Dad and three kids,

Buckled in on summer vacation.
Childhood memories created
Every stop along the way,

Grand Canyon, Four Corners,
Durango, Royal Gorge.
Hailstorm in Cortez,

Golf balls from God's back nine.
I thought: We need to get gas
Before we can vomit at the

Summit of Pikes Peak.
Nebraska, the wide-skied Platte,
Stones only an inch deep.

I couldn't drown if I tried.
Rambling on, Davenport,
Rock Island, Mississippi mud.

I can't remember if we hit
Missouri coming or going.
Mark Twain and Hannibal's caves.

Three boys, 7, 4 and almost 2.
Insanity in a station wagon,
Stop touching me, roll down the

Window. I'm going to put my
Hand in the cloud. Mom,
How did you do it?

The license plate game:
40 states and counting.
District of Columbia,

We're still searching for you.
Quietude came when her boys
Faded into the aluminum-hued

Vinyl backseats, brains awash
With new geographic destinations,
Maps, reservations, cities,

Steamboats and ferries too.
Dad, Afro trimmed, steadfast
behind the wheel, eyes peeled,

Pavement rising day after day.
Toledo, Ohio, Uncle Homer and
Aunt Rosa, Lake Erie, Perry and me

New York. We don't go to the City.
Summer of Sam, we never heard.
We don't reach Toronto, the stated goal,

But the Maid of the Mist served us
Well. We don't go over the falls
In a barrel. You could cross

Without a passport then.
When it hailed again at Fort George,
We scrambled under reinforced logs,

Waiting for the weather to pass
So we could pile into the Aspen
And dream again. The sanctity

Of the open road: We were disciples.
National Parks and the Rockies our gospel.
Our family Truckster our steed.

Another ferry ride, gliding atop
The rippling crests of Lake Michigan.
Homeward bound. Everything blurred.

The exuberance of brothers fighting
In the passenger seats, the confines of
Our young age, the Kansas prairie,

The silos and amber waves of grain.
At Garden of the Gods, I skinned my knee.
The blood stained the orange rocks.

I cried in pain but grew another scar,
Knowing I couldn't relive this saga.
I've forgotten what day it was

When we returned. Sunny, I bet.
The traffic, the smog welcomed us
With the wheezing and the coughs.

I don't fret. We, the family of five,
Are in that Aspen right now,
Forever in the memory dimension,

Looking for change between the cushions,
Little boys imploring truckers to blow the horn.
While I conspire with a family of my own.

IMPUNITY

I just need a little impunity.
Like a reprieve from a coffee spill.
Some time to sublimate the
Darker urges geared for pleasure.
Happiness is my responsibility.
Dignity, fealty, a break from reality.
Recess from life, not a departure.
The difference is the keyhole,
The passageway to sanity.
I'll come back when I'm ready.

THE FAR SIDE OF TIME

If time is an arrow,
Can you pierce my heart
Any gentler?
At the end of the line,
Scrubbed and rearranged,
Shun the wax of nostalgia.
Focus on the present facts.
I love you. You love me.
There's no guarantee
These sentiments will
Continue to the
Far side of time.
That moment is now,
The cogent state.
You don't need a gift
To express it, a mandated
Divestment of time and energy.
You only need believe
That the end is a lie,
The current instant: truth.
Create your verity every day.

WHERE DO LETTERS GO AFTER THEY'RE READ?

Where do letters go after they're read?
Letters. Handwritten.
Does anyone remember those?
Some saved, some discarded,
Your quivering heart decides
The moment, the hour, the fashion.
Burned by a blue-tipped match,
Returned to a trinket box,
Bloodshed from a wayward poke
From a letter opener bought in Calcutta.
Some are memorized, some forgotten.
All are hated, banal or praised.
Perhaps there's a dead letter society
For undeliverable missives meant for
An unknowing patron, a lover, a general.
Santa Claus? He has enough trouble.
The answer to the question of the moment
Lies in the deceptive land known as the
Bare truth, the truth hidden deep within
That nobody sees, hears or suspects.
Step One: Open.
Step Two: Read.

Step Three: Follow through on a decision
Born sometime just before Step One
When you ascertain the sender,
but during the drama of Step Two
When words make their case.
Waste basket at the ready.
A desk or drawer, or under your pillow.
Its destiny intertwined with yours.
Where do you go after you've read?

BLUE TEARDROPS

The stranger came from a distant world,
1976, sometime around then.
He landed in a canyon, next to a river.
It was polluted, full of beer cans, condoms,
And other gross earthborn totems,
Campers, having sex by a raft.
He walked into the nearest town,

Transformed into a beautiful woman.
They treated her different at the bar.
Can I buy you a drink ma'am, only darker.
They scarred her temporary human skin,
While a commercial appeared on TV.
Something about the environment.
They closed and locked the door,

The loggers' laughs sealed in the alien's brain.
When they finished, leaving the stains
Of lust in a grungy back room, she didn't cry.
She rose, anointed in the sins of man.
She snuck into the back seat of a
Blue pickup, listening to Marvin Gaye.
She jumped out 400 miles later,

Landed, prone, near another river,
This one ordained the Rio Grande.
A Navajo woman came to her aid,
Washed her face, gave her new clothes.
They sang outside her hogan,
Eyes glued to the Milky Way while
Bicentennial celebrations vanished.

The woman painted her visitor's face
In indigo, beautiful streaks like claws.
Time passed before their hoops,
Past, present and future in a fever dream.
When sunset came, the two women
Watched another body rise,
They called her Sentinel Moon.

They stared for hours until the stranded woman,
The one with the newest pain, changed,
Became a man again. He rose,
Kissed his colorful companion,
Transferring all his knowledge,
How to save the world, how to brave eternity.
The night bled into sunrise as

A monolithic mesa sailed into the cosmos.
The alien was no longer here.
But if you look closely, some nights
Blue teardrops flow across
The solemn lunar bird,
Who watches the global cinema
Play over and over again.

I FUCKING LOVE IT

The sun is out. So are the girls.
Polka dots and matching hearts,
Colors whirled into a swirl,
A confection of spirits,
Sweets and thrills.
I'm riding Pharaoh's Fury.
Up, down, swinging high.
Manhattan's menagerie.
The mélange of sights
Engender impurity,
Small business owners,
Landlords and flicks.
Keep stirring the batter,
Flesh out the lumps.
I'm too busy experiencing,
Bathing in the pleasures
Of our earthly prison.
Too much, too soon?
Temperance is hard to learn.
You don't have to like it.
You don't have to partake.
Don't judge my quest for
Blue jeans, brown eyes and boots.
Friday, in cahoots, smiles a wicked

Grin. The city, my lover,
Recognizes my plight.
Paint the town red.
No, I prefer blue.
Blue positions, impressive
Inclinations. When will it end?
This Machiavellian machine,
Ascendance and passion.
Where are you when I need you?
Absconded in some hotel room.
Empty bottles and clothes
Litter the languishing floor.
Let's scream it in unison: Inebriation.
I continue, quite simply put,
Decadence, I fucking love it.

THE COSMOS IS IN LINE AT IN-N-OUT

Palm trees have never seen better fries.
The grease, the grill, the California sun,
Potatoes perfectly salted and peeled
While we zoom toward oblivion,
Whistle with the Santa Ana wind.
Traffic, smog, taste eternal.
Everyone waits with a song,
A magnetic lullaby of happiness.
The cashier is everyone's friend.
We're all rapacious fiends inbound,
Long, turbulent flight from JFK,
First stop on the way home from LAX.
Mom and Dad. No money in
My pocket, change in the cup holder,
And the San Gabriel Mountains' wink.
Not even Puffy Taco is this sublime.
Lakers, Dodgers, Kings.
Post-game memories lie in wait.
No matter how long the queue.
Fans are alongside you,
Within their own universe,
Communing at the burger chapel.

The sky turns pink, orange.
Night alights. The stars align.
We know this to be true.
The cosmos is in line at In-N-Out,
Thinking the same thing:
I've been gone for far too long.

WET PAINT

Fill my mind with fluids,
Talk of textures and still life,
Rivers of landscapes and
Pointillist purviews
Awash in your perspective.
Touch me with your brush,
Filtering light into all
The dark places that
Need some tender love,
That need oozing oils,
Cascading down my body's canvas,
That need a salve of understanding.
Stand bare to our souls,
As we spiral into a tapestry
Of cosmic mixtures,
Relive our greatest secrets.
Motionless, I pose for hours,
Radiant and proud, then
Fall to my knees and drink,
Bathed in your wet paint.

THE FREEDOM OF A DARK BEDROOM

Sacred breaths. Our bodies slowly rise,
Our bosoms vibrating earth.
I, here with you in the middle of our night,
This beautiful prison we want to immortalize
Because we are the world's greatest lovers.
We fit like a sensuous puzzle.
It started with a simple desirous request.
It continues through the darkness
In an unmade bed, your kiss.
Your touch in hidden places,
Moves barely visible in the moonlight,
The lunar power of your immaculate face,
Your lips, full, with a hint of lavender,
That stains my skin while we build steam.
Kiss me again. I'll kiss you in return,
One long coital embrace, flesh pressed firm.
In the black, past midnight, we are free,
Greek deities changing form.
We are flowing water. We sigh endlessly.
You must have me. I must have you.
And as we dare to go deeper, we
Plunge into the pleasurable ether.

THE MUD PUDDLE

They say it doesn't rain in L.A.
The clouds don't work there.
The sun penetrates the June gloom,
Overcast skies rarely last, yet
Sometimes, once in a blue moon,
A storm born on the Pacific
Aimed for a roof gutter on a
Backyard garage on Light Street,
Back when I was a kid,
Before marital quarrels,
Before white hairs appeared.
It was a joyous occasion,
A cause for celebration.
I darted out the sliding glass door,
Behind which I had monitored progress,
My childlike wonder at the latest
Great Lake that formed from the runoff.
The more it rained, the greater
My imagination grew.
Leaves became ocean liners,
Twigs, tugboats, and drips, dreams.
Rain, rain please stay.
Don't go away some other day.
The depression made—I was nature's pupil—

No more than a few inches deep.
I could play for hours in a raincoat and
Track mud into the house and hear
My mother's groans. Take off your shoes!
Those days didn't last; they never do,
Faded into the corridors of memory.
There is a little boy somewhere,
Eyeing the clouds above, waiting,
Ready to spring forth, adulthood banished.
I am that boy, hidden inside,
Splashing in the puddle of life.

THE CONSTITUTION WILL NOT ENFORCE ITSELF

I hold this truth to be self-evident:
The Constitution will not enforce itself.
It won't bend to the whims of the inactive,
It will die in the grasp of the wicked,
Burn in its secure D.C. sealant.

Are we wrong in the assumption it is right?
Left alone, the uneducated won't know.
The document should be a pillar,
An end-all-be-all. Yet it isn't.
It must be executed, protected.

Sign your name on the dotted line,
The proclamation from colonial reclamation.
Let its size give you infamy until
Small hands with similar speciousness
Flaunt your almighty ideas.

We The People must abide, stay vigilant.
Divide and conquer is not the ticket.
Ballot box, citizens united. Ratify.
Big Brother is watching, marching in tune.
The Constitution will not enforce itself.

CITY OF CLONES

Out in the desert, past the ruined city,
Lies a beacon sending hope,
For the humans who didn't float.
City of Clones.

It's gleaming spires pierce the sky,
Protecting the specimens within.
They bathe in humanity's folly.
City of Clones.

They are Earth's guardians now.
They don't know their future,
The parents who gave them perfection.
City of Clones.

Destined for the stars, maybe Mars.
Who will teach them nature's rules?
Who will build the needed schools?
City of Clones.

Eggs and donors, an oasis of DNA,
From the mothers Daddy didn't know,
Sons and daughters waiting to grow.
City of Clones. City of Clones. City of Clones.

OL' RUSTY

1911: a year of golden shores.
Of brass futures, pomp
And heirloom circumstance.
The saxophone born to blow.
"In the Mood" and sassafras.
A plain instrument, at first,
Gleaming from a Georgia
Window. Its percussions
Waiting to be played.
In colored hands.
Jim Crow. Rag free.
First father, then son,
Then grandson, then great-grandson.
The museum of musical dreams
Beckons. Ol' Rusty granted
An indelible spotlight,
A clarion call. A family tree
Extends its branches like
Musical notes reaching
For an infinite sky.
Grandfather's gift.
Pads and spit.

Jazz writ large.
Love in the key of forever.
The genealogical vision.
Ol' Rusty we bow to thee.

"Ol' Rusty" first appeared in *Dime Show Review*, Volume 3, Issue 2 (2019)

LITTLE ETERNITIES

Everything is a wonder,
A concept without a clock.
These delicacies of childhood,
Looking both ways
Before crossing the street,
Running uphill to catch a
Butterfly or dandelion seeds,
Small voices and laughter,
Deliriously infectious, they are
Masters of the unchecked urge
To explore all in their sight,
Daughters wild, life's spark.
At some point they'll realize.
Someday they'll come of age.

Each moment, future's bridge,
A token fulfilled, a passport
To their land, where
Little eternities are the rule.
Each destined discovery,
Fuel, an ongoing school.
Love is no mystery.
It's there in their eyes,
In the glow of Mom and Dad,

In the fires of morphing minds.
Bask in their sunlight,
Learn from their wisdom.
When that distant day comes,
We will all be young.

THE FIRST DEAD AMERICAN

The bones could be anywhere.
Undiscovered, unrecognized,
American bones. The first Americans.
But let me digress, clean up the books.
America isn't a place on a map,
The fourth continent, "found" by Amerigo.
It's an idea. It's the people who
Came before, the indigenous souls,
The Africans in chains, the people
Who crossed the Bering Sea,
The railroad workers in Promontory,
It's the ghosts who built her,
Raised her from the floor.
It's founders and immigrants;
They are one and the same.
Crispus Attucks, Chief Joseph,
The Iroquois. Unmarked graves
Of their ancestors. Some known,
Most unnamed in history's tomes.
Their bones are everywhere:
The shores of Virginia, Jamestown,
Roanoke, Plymouth Rock.
Boston's tea party, another subterfuge,
Dressed like natives.

They couldn't even be honored
In the dark of night. Birth of a nation.
No taxation without representation.
No reclamation without reparation.
Manifest destiny, go west young man.
Take more people, take more land.
Until the first dead American
Becomes the last.

RED LAMPSHADE
AGAINST A DARK SKY

Red lampshade against a dark sky,
You, my wayward warden of the night.

Clouds summon their own wind,
Gray streaks backlit by bolting blue.

It is a quiet street.
There are no other lights.

If there are, I don't notice,
For reverie tangles me,

Your attractive sins, your
Distracting full-throated pleasures,

Your stark rouge. I trace your shadow
As it floats across the room,

Raises the temperature on pain,
And mocks the coming storm.

I stand, visions enthralled.
Rats dance past, smirking,

Leaving their truculent tears.
I want to move on, but can't,

Mesmerized by your radiant square,
A window emitting mystery,

An artificial light against my sorrow.
You say we walk two different paths.

The world fades into utter darkness.
I have no concept of time

Until a dog barks and his owner
Steps knowingly on my shoe.

I feel latent sensation, a
Malicious moth converging,

Look up and see your nude form.
The silent laugh, as you

Close the curtains.
I picture you masturbating

Just to make me cry,
To elevate a rat's shrieks

Higher than mine.
All I desire is your fiery glow,

Still visible behind the doomed tapestry.
I pause, did we share anything real?

I filter the best moments,
Confident in the notion that

I don't know the truth.
The lampshade flickers off.

I, adrift, ponder my *own* thoughts.
At least I know I exist.

TWO HUMAN SOULS

I was walking in Whenville,
The capital of aspirations,
When I spied your eyes.
You claim you spied mine.
Details lost in history.
The point is clear.
We are two earthly humans,
Cast among billions of
Other earthly humans.
The astronomical odds
Of maintaining equilibrium,
Besides the simple fact
We crossed strings,
Didn't deter a destined future.
The power filled the sky,
And the abstract notion of harmony
Transformed into a crystal.
Able to shatter, able to absorb light.
We exchanged rings, wed true.
We two, then three, then four.
We're on the ship of creativity,
Hurtling toward the unknown.
Yet unconcerned. Dying.
Our quantum consciousness

Dovetails into the universe.
Where it becomes,
One.

FOREIGN-BODY SENSATION

Jet fuel, a plume in the atmosphere.
Attack the next destination,
Conjuring a lover, or discovering
The kinks of a local accomplice.
Blue jeans and black shoes,
Black skirt, blue sweater,
Articles pressed then shed.
Cobblestone streets,
Blue walls in the blue pearl,
Beauteous beaches beset
By the sky in liquid form.
Zanzibar, Kamakura, Hvar.
Lands unfolding in secret.
Where everyone acts alone,
Surrounded by hundreds
Of other tourists,
Human beings being
Whoever they want to be.
Foreign bodies compressed in
Hotel suites, the maelstrom:
Passion with a dash of recklessness.
Danes, Swedes, Japanese girls,
Continents and Malian majesty,
Ebony and honey-dipped hips.

Diplomats of pleasure.
Weightless cities broker peace.
The clouds of the journey
Never remembered,
Only the succulent gash of hedonism,
The morning sensation. Nothing
Stuck in the eye except the scar
Of nubile partners, naked in the mirror.
The consequences pale in
Comparison; tomorrow is tomorrow.
Rhapsody reverberates
From Bangkok to Sofia
While the proud players
Return to mundane pursuits.
It was never supposed to last.

THE LAST OPPONENT

We are all daughters and sons of woman,
Born of mothers and mothers' mothers.
We walk this Earth and shine,
Some brighter than others,
The ones tasked with the spotlight.
Some last minutes, others, days,
Weeks, months, years, decades,
Centuries, until we are thrilled.
Some pick up tools of science,
Music, religion, law, while
Some pick up a basketball,
A tool of an equal sort,
A dimpled globe to zap images
Around a greater globe, shadowed
By the aura of the Creator,
Set in purple and gold,
The color of royalty.
We all have regal blood,
Quanta with vast potential,
Like children, among the nine,
Among the mourning many.
We are all a great opponent,
Overcoming rivers of tears,
When sad, when we fail,

Then rising from the floor,
Running the lanes, boxing out,
Smiling into the cup
When we win the championship,
Passing knowledge from lips
Doused with champagne.
This life is our title plane,
Yet not the final 24-second clock.
We triumph in the unknown hour,
Magnificent creatures blessed by death:
The last opponent to be destroyed.
And we check into the timeless game.

ACKNOWLEDGMENTS

First and foremost, thank you to my family, especially to my wife—for putting up with my idiosyncrasies and writing indulgences—and our beautiful daughters: this is part of your legacy. I hope you find some solace, meaning and understanding in these words. Thank you, Mom and Dad and my brothers. I feel like it's still the Summer of '77 and we're all driving around the continental U.S. (and Canada) in the Dodge Aspen. And thank you to many, many others: Robson Garcia Jr., Chilembwe Mason; Jimmy Chan, Hiromi Saeki, Chi Mac, Faisal Azam, Erica Velis, John Plenge, Paul Gutierrez, Dimitry Leger, Naomi Castillo, Lisa Darling, Karen Lee, Ancel Bowlin, Scott Hevesy, Jaramay Aref, everyone at *Sports Illustrated*, Richard Demak, Larry Mondi, Joy Birdsong, Natasha Simon, Susan Szeliga, Karen Meneghin, Diane Smith, Gabe Miller, John Shostrom, Pam Roberts, Kevin Kerr, Tony Scheitinger, Jill Jaroff, Nancy Ramsey, Bernice Rohret, Joan Rosinsky, Anne Vallersnes, Sonja Kiefer, Bettina Meetz, Linda Bukasen, Julia Luu, João Serejo, Kevin Gidden, Claudia Ancalmo (and everyone from Disneyland), Brian Jaramillo, Jennymar, Mrs. Pell, Lars Anderson, Tracy Mothershed, Simone Procas, Judy Margolin, Gary Garrison, Andrea Woo, Albert Chen, Lisa P. LeGrand, Andrew Paredes, Jackie Bergman, Mike Johnson, Leslie Bornstein, Julian Rozzell Jr., Seevon Chau and family, Marina and Jason Anderson of Polgarus Studio, everyone at the Minskoff Theater, everyone at St, Matthias, The Bias Family, The Pitts Family, The Smith Family, The Takahashi Family, The Tanaka Family, The Lao Arpasuwong Family, our Brooklyn friends and neighbors, The Okitsu Family, The Cervantes Family; The Sigur Family and everyone on Light Street; Willie Joe Philbin and The Philbin Family, my friends, fraternity brothers and football teammates at the University of Arizona. If I have forgotten anyone, it was not intentional. You have all helped me on my journey. In addition, thank you to anyone who has ever written, read or listened to a poem, and to those of you who are thinking about it. I believe the definition of poetry is subjective. It can be a single word, or a 50,000-line epic tale of free verse, or a painting, a glance, a film, a photograph, a sculpture, an amazing design, a play, a lover, a glass of milk or the glint in your children's eyes. Poetry is life and vice versa. I hope you enjoy this latest collection. Thank you the reader, the watcher, the seeker, the human being.

Kelvin C. Bias, New York City, Feb. 14, 2020

OTHER WORK
BY KELVIN C. BIAS

MILKMAN (Novel)

What happens when everyman Calder Boyd starts to lactate? The Manhattanite becomes a media cause célèbre nicknamed the Milkman and old and new problems spill forth. The son of a former NBA star and a Norwegian artist, Calder copes with his strained marriage, losing his copywriting job at a boutique ad agency, a male-empowerment espousing mailman and a porn-star performance artist who wants to exploit him. He also deals with his late father's legacy and his wife's past indiscretion—all while breastfeeding their newborn daughter. Calder eventually becomes a pawn in the battle between a feminist organization and a militant men's society as he tries to become a better husband and man. The Fourth Estate, sex, art, love, memory, marriage and family converge during the snowiest winter on record in this commentary on contemporary American fatherhood.

WHISPERS OF A DYING SUN (Poetry)

These poems represent the vestiges of man from the perspective of a distant future. Akin to radio signals, the remnants of humanity streak toward a black hole where art, politics, love, technology, philosophy, science and the yearning for eternity accrete. Prophetic, stoic, polyphasic, the words disassemble and recombine on the other side in search of a new sun. I hope these poems find a closer home in your personal universe, heard but you're unsure of their origin, like whispers.

SEXOPOLIS: POEMS ON LOVE AND SEX

Love is a liberation, an act, a rebellion, a restriction, a communion. This poetry collection covers the universal topics of love and sex. From erotic to platonic and from marital to familial, love comes in many forms. We don't always get it, but we all crave it.

IMMACULATE DUST: LOVE POEMS

This poetry collection delves headlong into the world of love. Encompassing the realms of dream, fantasy and reality, the poems intend to engender not just love, but more pointedly, lovemaking. Lust. Love. Languor. These are three states of mind and body before, during and after the most pleasant poetry of human interaction: consented sex. We all possess desire and we are all made of dust. Immaculate dust.

21 PARTICLES OF ETERNITY (Poetry)

Is eternity a quantifiable entity? An existence that can be divided into smaller particles, assembled and disassembled like a puzzle? Can it be bent? Borrowed? Recycled? Eternity is elusive. It constantly seems beyond our grasp yet always within our reach. *21 Particles of Eternity* covers topics as disparate as Mars and pornography, and ranging from global warming and parenthood to politics and death. The poet posits this: perhaps there are hidden portals where eternity can be glimpsed for fleeting moments, and the quest to find them brings meaning. How many particles will you find?

ABOUT THE AUTHOR

Kelvin C. Bias is a journalist, novelist, poet, filmmaker, raconteur and aesthete. However, his most important moniker is father. He lives in Brooklyn with his wife and daughters.

If The Sky Is Awake is his fifth poetry collection. Connect with Kelvin on Instagram & Twitter: @archivezero

www.ingramcontent.com/pod-product-compliance
Lightning Source LLC
LaVergne TN
LVHW051522070426
835507LV00023B/3257